I0756348

FINISHING LINE PRESS
www.finishinglinepress.com

Rollercoaster of Life

poems by

Phyllis Carito

Finishing Line Press
Georgetown, Kentucky

Rollercoaster of Life

Copyright © 2026 by Phyllis Carito
ISBN 979-8-89990-389-2 First Edition
All rights reserved under International and Pan-American Copyright Conventions. No part of this book may be reproduced in any manner whatsoever without written permission from the publisher, except in the case of brief quotations embodied in critical articles and reviews.

ACKNOWLEDGMENTS

Previously published poems:
Orchard Beach, Bronx NY (*Boomer Lit Mag*)
Heat & Normal Anomaly (*North of Oxford*)
I wear sensible shoes for the journey (*In Other Words, Anthology*)
The Way Love Destroys You (*Passager Journal*)
Bodies (*Inkwell Review*)
Hike in the Rockies (*Rockvale Review*)
Train to Penn Station (*Stone Highway Review*)

Publisher: Leah Huete de Maines
Editor: Christen Kincaid
Cover Art: Phyllis Carito (San Francisco, CA)
Author Photo: Patricia Fecher (Lisbon Portugal)
Cover Design: Elizabeth Maines McCleavy

Order online: www.finishinglinepress.com
also available on amazon.com

Author inquiries and mail orders:
Finishing Line Press
PO Box 1626
Georgetown, Kentucky 40324
USA

Contents

These poems were first printed in barely a whisper* (2010) or The Stability of Trees in the Winds of Grief** (2019) Chapbooks published by Finishing Line Press

This book is dedicated to friends for whose support and encouragement I am ever grateful.

Happiness is when what you think, what you say,
and what you do are all in harmony.

Mahatma Gandhi

Prologue:

Poem: My Life

It was a very, very long time ago
In a place I used to exist

It was a very, very short distance
From my life to the risk

It was chance and fate to take
Into the mix the way to fix

Orchard Beach, Bronx NY

two city buses getting there
sweat soaked
dragging our bags across hot sand
finding a square of space
sitting on the woolen blanket
frying skin burning red
sand crystals in my cheese sandwich
plums and warm lemonade;
down to the water
she swam back and forth
breast stroke, side stroke
her white cap bobbing,
my feet sinking into the sand
sea weed floating around my legs
hot, blurry hot, dip down
stand back up
she had to be able to see you
waiting on the edge
you couldn't go past your knees
you couldn't swim
you couldn't swim
you silly girl
you couldn't swim away

Heat

Only when she must; sun down, she goes up
stairs into the heat where her mother's simmered all day
while her father chased shots down with beer
and only for as long as she must stay;
until she turns girl to woman—
steadily bleeds her monthly heat;
their begging unable to delay the clowns
and the acrobats from coming.
Already her mouth-watering for the Devil Dog's dry dark
And sweet creamy insides, sticky on her fingers, sweat
like the warmth adhering blouse to chest, gummy between her legs.
The heat swipes at random intervals
in flashes percolating in her chest,
like lava slides spilling across her neck
lighting two cheek blazes,
fire throbbing at her temples, sweater on, sweater off—
she tastes the temptations from grimy hands,
she laughs although they warned she'd be crying;
the man who picked up her scent won't forgive her for his desire.

Believer

Mom joined with dad again.
Buried in a Bronx cemetery
lined with stones and sections
of old Italian relatives.
Monuments shoulder to shoulder
leave no room for new arrivals.
Spanish names to be etched. You know,
they've moved into the neighborhood.

Mom always had high hopes
for a wonderful place, a being
better than setting mouse-traps
every night, waiting by the window
for me to wander home.
She offered daily prayers
rolling the beads across her fingers,
aiming to secure that heaven.

I would distress her:
"Doubting Thomas, why don't you
believe in miracles?"

Shoes too worn to be worn

I miss my children
as children, taking my time away
from buying comfortable shoes.

At night I'd stretch my toes,
walk barefoot into their bedrooms
see features melted into dreams,
blankets tucked to their chins,
bodies preparing for the next spurt

uncovering two shoe-size growth.
We got used to callused heels, blistered
toes, sweaty sneakers, rejected pumps,
flip-flops to hiking boots. All worn.

Our home turned to a storage shed
housing outdated computers, Woody Guthrie
music, prom dress, 5 years of Sports Illustrated—
he had to have, every ski-lift ticket
from every mountain she every skied.

All worn. Should we have started over again—
What did we grow while they grew?

I have to buy a closet full of new shoes.

I wear sensible shoes for the journey

In unmapped territory
weighted down with the past,
seeking inward markers
for my essential self

propelled journey,
I must count on kindness of strangers
who stop to fix my flat tire,
friends appearing over tree tops,
great red-tailed hawks
drawing my eyes upward,
or strength sensed at my side,
shadow of gentle moving giraffe
tipping lightly, nudging me along.

Keep breathing in, blue sky, crisp air,
walk unsteady steps through
the eclipse bearing
light and dark miseries,
shedding old weights,
readying my heart to give again.

It's another

(For Corey)

hot day and there'll be another.
I'll watch the flowers wilt.
I'll struggle to get out
of the chair, to push myself.
I wonder if it's so hard because
we can't get behind ourselves—
two solid hands on our shoulders
—to push.

It's another attempt to reach her
and I'll attempt to reach her again.
She's my daughter.
I won't ever give up. No
wonder it's so hard.
She's my daughter—
thickheaded—as my mother
told me I was.

It's another lovely escape,
to plant flowers, hope
for a bouquet, a moment's
reprieve that we make
for ourselves
because without it,
we can't make another attempt
at living.

Morning Stars

Morning stars across the sky
in my window   as I lie
charting stars to freckles
of paths across   as I live
often lost
I need a map
laid out with every road
I can take
every way I can go
sign posts along the way
for the high road
for the long stretch of valley
for the hidden turns
lift my head
for my future   a next phase
I need a driver
a horn blower
a lights' on   creating
of a mood
stars twinkling
in the morning calm

Coffee

for Diane

Perking in the pot, heart jolting
cups of insomnia   roasting
Follow the aroma—pungent, nutty,
seeking, heart leaping

all habit, routine
have yours with a cigarette?
heartbreak? eggs over easy?
in the kitchen, or in the café,

when it's bitter walk away.

The Way Love Destroys You

You flick the night into the gutter
pass on the strong mints.
In the cotton mouth morning
you remember what you tried to forget.

You have to give up smoking;
the spell and spark, uncountable packs a day,
struck matches through the heat of body,
living so long in the curling smoke
sucking in every sorrow,
clouding your head
with every promise of refreshment.

It's time for you, to give up smoking, at least
cut down, leave the pack on the counter, walk away.
you'll still have your stash spots—to inhale
in a crowded room, or one drag and toss
out the car window—
stains detailing love's cravings.

House

A house drove by today
In two perfect halves
Escorted by flashing lights
Leaving no room for others
To pass, to move, to leave.
A house ready to be split
Whenever they sever
the relationship.

Umbra

why must you live in the umbra
there is light left to shine on you

why are you staying absent when
my eyes want to look on you

after the eclipse doesn't the moon shine brighter
we have a place under the moon together

I let you go, and then I wait for you
I ache for you so, then, you give me one breath

I breathe it in and the light begins to warm me,
then, you retreat, the light goes into shadow

why must you live in the umbra
and leave me hanging on the dark side of the moon?

Mid-winter

I left the light on
For the mouse in the kitchen.
I left my socks on.
I just wanted to get a few weeks sleep;
Then set the trap for the mouse,
Calculate my taxes,
Remove the lint from the drier;
Decide how to live without you

Magic

It's a slight of heart
And I can't catch you

I'm in need of a tourniquet

I know you can dazzle me
With colorful scarves
Or break me in half.

Do you want me to disappear?

I'm scraping at the black box
But I can't get out

Metaphors for a Love Story

I fell into a dream
Where it rained cats and dogs
And I waited for the other shoe to drop
That shoe on the other foot,
Knowing you can't teach an old dog new tricks
Or warm yourself on a blanket of snow or a sheet of rain.
I should have broken it off
Clean as a whistle;
Been the fat lady who sang
And nipped it in the bud.

My left arm is numb

My left arm is numb
and my fingers cold,
I could say it is from
an injury,
I could say I don't know,
maybe just a falling asleep.

It seems it should be
low, but it is high
blood pressure.

I could say because they
have all the answers,
And I'm tired of asking
all the questions.

I could say because my heart
is broken and has stopped
circulating blood, warmth,
energy to and fro.

And this seems to be the way the blood
pumps now, sluggish with pulse
slowed. Aged, and carrying loss
and no arms any longer around me.

Where are my blue skies?

Are they hovering over the evergreens?
Are they breaking through on the other side of the maples?
Are they in his eyes?

Woven in the words I choose, the colors move
from the blues of childhood
to the blue of star filled skies.

Is there a place for me under the canopy
of peaceful places, evergreens scented sweet
with a companion to greet?

Clear sight and cuddled tight
to bring me blue skies
to hold all day and night.

A sense of senses

begins with orb of eye
that takes in light
telescopes to far and wide
or pinpoints to specs—
the tick buried in the dog's fur,
the splinter needled under skin.
Can the eyes alone glimpse
love before it's known?

Taste can't lick the moon.
The tongue's stimulation
is cinnamon, cardamom, cayenne,
coated with ice cream
or warmed with coffee
bitter on the side, with a sweet tip,
sour throwing up when you are sick.

What of breathing and smelling,
schnozzle that whiffs
not only acrid and sweet,
but pores releasing fear.

What of what we do not hear?
We misinterpret, we misconstrue,
we do not hearken, fine-tuned
like canine or owl—we're given
to sticking fingers in our ears.

Tattoos

Hearts, stars, a third eyeball
the name of a beloved dead
sleeves of wolves, crown arms
encircled bird wings cross back of necks
swirls of words up calves to thighs
forever messages of pinpointed pricks
needle by needle
celebrated indelible markings

Beauty worth pain
for the pledge of love
for the cry of loss;
art as the history
of all your living—
following the body shape
emphasizing the collar bone
displaying on the knuckles
be it—h.a.t.e. or l.o.v.e.

Bodies

So we have a place to pump the blood
Veins to the heart, carotid arteries to the brain
Circling and consequentially bringing
A rush to hands, a flush to face.
So we have a suitcase full of parts
That brain matter, 3 pounds worth,
Can orchestrate in tiny impulses, nerves endings
Twitching faster than we can read this line.
So we have colon waste exhaust
From intestines running snake roads south;
Every organ squeezed, against maltreat feed
In expanded stomachs, or uterus times twenty
So we can reproduce ourselves.

It is all here in their donated death
To be living statues scalped of protective skin
Chopped into delicacies of scientific explanations,
Did they all have good teeth, few broken bones?
We find our breaks—elbow radius, shattered ankle;
Our beat diseases—stone blocking our gall bladder;
Where the cancer was cut out.

When the skin was peeled did their spirit escape?
No soulful look in their frozen eyes
No pain, furrowed brows, or grimaces
For where their Achilles tendon is snipped
Or their lungs are blackened.

Tabernacles of our living honored
So we visualize bone connects, muscles,
Tendons contracting, relaxing,
The flex and beat of body;
So we can hold hands.

Sensory Overload

cacophony of German
Japanese
Spanish
taxi horns hawking vendors
flaring nostrils garlic and sweat
above ground bus fumes
underground screeching subway
perfume garbage on the curb
Broadway bright homeless begging
pickpockets press close pocketbook alley sales
people pouring out of every doorway
around every corner eyes alert
pound the pavement clutch yourself
the city never sleeps never sleeps

Normal Anomaly

For R&S
"...as way leads on to way" The Road Not Taken, Frost

Doctors find anomaly in body parts that don't
match their anatomy charts and won't
when the normal function is challenged,
when the deviation appears,
doesn't meet the probability unless
the paths are rerouted for task.

We find anomaly of channels when we leap
from a distortion hidden deep
in daily patterns of our lives,
concealing true identity with social expectation
until we come upon a bend,
an incongruity from a supposed anticipation

as if our eyes are on upside down, we reach,
perchance we fly above the weighted beliefs
making all the normal prospects turn their heads.

Righting Reflexes

Our colossus still stands
at our sea-washed, sunset gates, her torch
still symbolizing—welcome—your tired,
your poor, your huddled masses yearning;
a life-saving response to our families
once come to these shores
with the feeling of falling off the edge
between their old and new lives.

Our declaration still speaks
"life, liberty, and the pursuit
of happiness," offering safety
for our welcome masses;
feeling the imbalance,
uncertainty; the need
for love to trump hate.

We need a righting reflex
some transformation,
pinned with our belief
that an open heart
can be a call for hope;
twist, and recover, like a cat—
landing us on our feet.

Terror

The world is crying
and we can't dry all the tears,
the pools are overflowing
and we can't turn the spigot off,
can't find the valve through miles
and miles of piping mired
in years and years of anger and hurt,
twisted with the callings of gods
tangled in the web of religions' names
lost in the politics of human greed.

The world is crying
and we can't turn the spigot off,
our forever is coming close to an end
and we can't save the world
by killing nature, neighbor, and reason,
twisted with the callings of gods
tangled in the web of religions' names
lost in the politics of human greed—
how do you spell human beings
in a drowning demise of hate?

After September 11, 2001

We can't test courage cautiously.
Fire has been driven
from a crystal blue sky
deep into our bellies.

We can't ask for our lives back.
Taking theirs is not enough
to alleviate our fear, strengthen
our core with new resolve.

It is not something new
we search in the rubble for,
it is remembering
why and how we began, uniting
into states, minds embracing freedom.

How To Make America Great Again
(A Villanelle)

In making America great again,
First admit that it has always had flaws;
Point out the fakers as vile and foul.

The states to unite, must work to regain
Diversity as strength and at the core
In making America great again.

The good people shining bright to attain
American democracy in awe,
Recognize the fakers as vile and foul.

The racists and misogynists complain
And learn, too late, they created this war.
Not making America great again.

Reach past the past and find what must pertain
For building a new trust from shore to shore
Recognize the fakers as vile and foul.

And you, dear Americans, shine humane
In your exchanges narrow and broad.
In making America great again,
Refuting fakers as vile and foul.

My eyes

From my broken heart to the parents of children lost at Sandy Hook

my eyes are tired
even when I wake

sometimes so many tears fall
that they are squeezed dry

sometimes the brightness hurts
with all the unhappiness behind my eyes

I remember
my eyes used to smile

Instructions for children going to school in the USA

Leave your lunch box home,
bring your bleeding kit.
Don't worry about learning
history, you're living it.

Your parents might be prone
to have you wear a flak-jacket
When you practice how
to place a tourniquet
on your classmate,
so, she/he/they won't
be fated to bleed out.

The shooter doesn't know you,
has been sold a bill of goods
that twists his mind, to hate, to kill.
Your parents would protect you
if they could.

Don't worry your teacher
will be there
to practice the emergency drill,
each time someone comes
near the classroom door.
Just remember, stop
learning, and drop to the floor.

Protect our children's childhood

Through the walls of the schools,
In the halls of the schools
Come the sounds of the children,
The squeaks of instruments being tuned,
The squeals of children running in the gymnasium,
And the giggles, giggles, giggles.

Protect our children's childhood.
They need to know their schools
Are not going to crumble,
That the sounds down the hall are
Not gunshots shattering the windows and walls.

Protect our children's childhood.
They need to learn something new each day,
To add, to build, to share,
With wonder in their eyes,
In their classrooms, in the halls
Paintings, and drawings, and visions explored;
Not signs on the emergency drill
And where to get your bleeding kit
And how to hit the floor.

Remember the photographs
Of schools in *those* countries—
Were continuous war,
A constant threat
Of guns, and fear, but not,
Our country. And what was
Left were schools crumbling down
And the children, their eyes vacant,
Not bright, no smiles, in those countries,
Not *our* country.

Protect our children's childhood.
Where children sit in a circle on the floor,
Cross-legged listening to a story,
With wonder in their eyes,

And whispers to each other,
And smiles to their teachers
And giggles, giggles, giggles.

Stop the gun access—NOW!

In and Out of Patience with the Chipmunk

He sticks his head out from under
the old wood pile tarp

A flash of reaction from us both
Another spot he's taking up—

What matter? There is no more
smoke coming from the chimney

The tarp is faded, lost its blue
Turned my care to gardens

There I clap my hands at him
and shred Zest or Irish Spring

Defer him from nibbling
on carefully spaced tulip bulbs

He scurries into his favorite pot
My oldest treasure from Grandpa's

A stone planter that once sat, side
to side with another on the porch steps

The chipmunk pops his head out
His cheeks no longer full

He's focused and consistent
While I linger on yesterday

Why? How? If only…
I toss another weed into the basket

Run through chores to be done
Recite Mary Oliver's "Wild Geese"

Pick flowers for the table
Watch him walk along the stone wall

Like a child would choose to do

Grackles, not raven or crow

I know the raven from Poe.
The crow that dances on one foot.
But these, slender blackbirds with
brown undertones and shiny blue heads
decorate my driveway with abstract art,
white blotches of scattered feces.
They gather in the pines and screech
to each other the day's events.
The porch is unusable during mating
season, the refuse littered everywhere,
including the featherless pink bellied song-
bird babies and Robin's broken blue shells.

I purchase a stone relief of a blackbird
and post it on my porch rail as a prayer,
hang bells and wind chimes
to keep the grackle flying wide—out
to the trees and field. We play this game
every spring, me trying to edge them
away from the house and bird feeders.
Then summer settles in and I'm searching
among the trees at empty nests, left
wondering where they've all gone.

Why not to get a cat

Feral cats take your hand outs
but still sharpen their claws on you.
What choice—captivity or supermarkets?
We've all lost the ability to hunt.

Cats seeking a home, I don't offer—
an environment for a live-in roommate—
of more lonely nights
prowling around while I'm sleeping.

Lahaina, Banyan Tree, August 8, 2023

I have heard the stories of so many humans
as they sat beneath my branches.
I have dropped new limbs to root
and extend my base. The native Hawaiians
embraced my growth and allowed
my spread to be a place for all to sit
in the shade of my foliage,
on benches, along paths.
My branches as foreground to the ocean,
background for visitors' photographs.

Three of these visitors sat along a center bench
in the park that is my home, where I am the only tree
since 1873 in the court yard square,
absorbing the sun and heat, and swaying
with the ocean breezes.
They call me Banyan, and they sit eating pineapple slush
and love *the wonder* they say I am.

The people of Lahaina call me Ohana.
The people of Lahaina who lived in paradise
with me—until the hell came upon us.
Wildfire over the mountain
and rushing down the street, blowing
through my leafy head and scorching
my many arms.

My deep roots shiver.

Hike in the Rockies

For Roland 1975-2017

I might have missed
the curved horns on his tilted head
or his heart-shaped hooves balanced
on the rock edge right above us,
if you hadn't circled me with your arm,
guided us a step back on the path.

The next moments frozen in time.
This bighorn sheep and our stunned stillness,
the exchanged looks of awe,
the quiet, the path not ours to claim.
How adept his wooly body turned
straight up that rock face
so quickly, and we so slowly moved on.

Ahead of me your strong legs, wool socks,
and LL Bean hiking boots,
your grandpa Cicchetti's broad shoulders,
your dark hair circling the nape of your neck.
You slowed down for me, to catch up,
took my hand to ascend to the spot
you wanted to share—
a mother and son vista.

Silence

on the open plain of long distances,
the morning sunlight reaching
around the jolting mesa,
the mitten butte standing in shadow,
its stratified silt, sand, and shale
hidden from site until the sun
spotlights it as I watch;
while far in the distance
a snow-covered mountain
rises beyond sage brush
and golden grass on Navajo red earth.
I hold a sandstone glittering with turquoise,
watch a hawk shadow across the Valley of the Rocks,*
          taking me to calmness, clearing my clutter
here in the valley of 160 million years ago.

*Tsé Bii' Ndzisgaii (Navajo)

Train to Penn Station

rushes along the river,
sun peeking out and in
sparkles dancing   darkening,
steel of bridges, wave caps,
bald headed eagle gliding   returning

to other train rides   your father
bringing you water from the pointed paper cup,
rocking, chugging of the train   interrupted

a town blurring by,
a swamp seeping by the river running
to the ocean,
a finback whale swallowing the Hudson   sleepy

rocked child, quiet and calm,
house along the edge to rest your head   live

with smoke stacks on the other bank?
storms that will crest   toss
a lone sailboat.

Riding Alone

In low light I left the house. Crows
were cleaning the road, the seeds sowed

in spring made a canyon of corn
that I drove through in a mourning

across the valley in a mist
longing for that which had been kissed.

Seeking in what new direction?
Brights blinding the intersection.

One way warning to watch my speed
Dare I cross the line, take the lead.

Find my way with windows let down
Seat-heater on, leaving this town.

Morning

I'm here for another morning
open my eyes to the soft light,
scan the family pictures, and art
feel the comfort of a warm bed
under the roof of my own home

There's no way to know if this day
Is the last of light before dark
beyond the living, we hold dear,
yet yearning for the afterlife
in this paradox way we live

Some say it is the mode of God
to have us question, but then nod
in the belief, that holds this faith,
others say, it's universal
energy that rules this planet

And all that matters is to live
when you are among the living
and hasten not to judge others
not to bring ruin to your own,
celebrate this day as given

Under Any Particular Scar

My sorrow for how deep the cut
My sorrow for the unsightly variance on the surface
Exposing the wound, hiding the hurt with undermined tissue.
My sorrow for wars lingering in the minds of men
My sorrow for homeless never getting a good night's sleep
For dreams turned nightmares, for dreams left undreamed
When the suffering causes anxiety
When the suffering causes despair.
My sorrow for the missed joys that are the prize of loss.
My sorrow for every day that needs to be treated with aloe, vitamin E,
Kindness to yourself where kindness was taken from your vocabulary.
My sorrow for every needed therapist who eases each eruption.
My sorrow for the scar on the underside.

Heading Over the Hill

Lighten your load
Be done with bulky baggage
Embrace simple satisfactions
Appreciate solitude

No platitudes to reach
Be content with:

The morning birds
Coffee and conversation
Dinner with friends
But afternoons alone

With more behind
And less ahead
Let go of uncertainty
You aren't yet dead

Live the consolation prizes
Swirling sublime days

Purple Clouds

I like purple clouds changing to gray
announcing the rain to wash away
my melancholy
I like wind at my back pushing me
along while it whistles a song
I like the dog that walks me every day
it's good to explore her way

I don't like whimsical
I don't like stagnant air
I don't like many people, *sorry to say*

I like patterns of trees on the hill side
I like roads that roam
I like the laughter of grandchildren
I like elephants and giraffes

Under the purple clouds
Across the one sky
On the one earth
that we share

Terminology: Old

Stiff and swollen fingers in the morning. That coughing all the time is annoying. Let the dog out. Cousin Phil came yesterday—all that talk about the past. You better make a list. Let the dog back in. It's just a tickle in the back of your throat. Is there something you've got to say? The kitchen floor must be washed. You won't get to that today. Where does the day go?

Start today with yoga. Maybe after that you can wash the kitchen floor. Cousin Phil isn't coming; he's too cheap to eat out. Where are we going, anyway? Must you leave the light on all day? Is there something you need to find? You need to make a list for the groceries. You haven't heard that hymn since the 50s. Just get out of the house. Walk the dog. Her nose sniffing the ground, your eyes on flag poles, steeples, and towering pines. Stay away from the crowds. Has your head been in the clouds?

As for your memory and not trying to relive the past, where are you going anyway? Did you forget? Not the losses. Is this what getting old offers? Acceptance of now, no promise of tomorrow. Acknowledge your accomplishments, but get out of the way for the innovators of today. Are you expected to become a shadow of yourself? All this thinking—how about drinking? You're not too old to love. You're not too old to eat pizza. You're not too old to care.

Phyllis Carito, MFA. A retired academic dean, she teaches creative writing through SUNY-CGCC, and workshops at local libraries, including the Roe Jan Library, and Kinderhook Memorial Library. Her published books include: *barely a whisper, The Stability of Trees in The Winds of Grief, Worn Masks, Travel Light* and *More Than Making Ends Meet.* Her sequel novel: *More Than A Feeling,* presented in mid-2025. Other fiction or poems in anthologies: *Wild Crone Wisdom; Gray Love; Gathering Flowers;* and literary magazines: *Passager Journal, Mediterranean Review, Persimmon Tree, Voices in Italian Americana, Inkwell Review, Vermont Literary Review, Rockvale Review, North of Oxford Literary Review* and *Boomer Lit Mag.*

This collection engages with all her senses over varied places and times. Sharing the process of writing with other authors, and the support of friends and readers is a joy of the writing process and she appreciates the encouragement and responses from readers.

Find reading dates and more on Phyllis Carito at Phylliscarito.weebly.com

www.ingramcontent.com/pod-product-compliance
Lightning Source LLC
LaVergne TN
LVHW090538110826
845146LV00003B/1155

* 9 7 9 8 8 9 9 9 0 3 8 9 2 *